Global Edition

Reprogram

Break the Loop,
Reclaim the Rhythm,
Retrn to You.

BY

DR.SAIF QAZI

Reprogram – Global Edition
© Dr. Saif Qazi, 2025
All rights reserved.

No part of this publication may be reproduced, stored, or transmitted in any form or by any means—electronic, mechanical, photocopying, recording, or otherwise—without prior written permission from the author, except for brief quotations used in reviews or academic work with proper attribution.

This is an original work. Any resemblance to actual persons, events, or published material is purely coincidental and unintentional.

This book is intended for educational and personal development purposes only. It is not a substitute for professional medical, psychological, or therapeutic advice. Readers should consult qualified professionals for individual health or mental wellness concerns.

Published for global distribution. Rights are reserved in all countries. Unauthorised reproduction, adaptation, or commercial use is strictly prohibited.

Ingram ISBN: 978-93-342-9607-5

MirrorVerse™ Publisihing

Editing & proof Reading : Zeenat Qazi

For rights, permissions, or speaking engagements:

✉ hello@drsaifqazi.in

www.drsaifqazi.in

First Global Edition – April 2025

DEDICATION

To the ones who held space when I couldn't hold myself.
To the hands that reached gently into my silence.
To those who stayed, not for answers but simply for presence.
To my loved ones, whose love felt like calm in the middle of a storm.
To my patients, who reminded me that healing often arrives in whispers.
To my sons, Tabish and Faiz, whose questions, laughter and quiet strength breathe life into these pages.
And to you, the reader. May these words be a mirror that helps you remember the truth of who you are.

Preface

We are not born with a manual for the mind.
We inherit patterns before we understand them.
We carry stories in our body long after the moment has passed.

As a physician, I have spent years listening to symptoms.
But beneath every symptom, I began to notice something deeper.
Unseen beliefs. Suppressed memories. Emotional signatures so old, they had no words.

I wrote *Reprogram* not to offer advice, but to offer a mirror.
Not to fix anyone, but to help people see how they were shaped—by experiences, culture, nervous system memory, and quiet patterns that run the show without being seen.

This book comes from two journeys.
One through science—neuroscience, psychology, trauma, and behaviour.
The other through the emotional terrain of being human—grief, shame, numbness, and eventually, clarity.

What you will find here is not a one-time read.
Each chapter is meant to be lived with.
There are ideas to reflect on, stories that might sound like your own, and practices that slowly shift your inner wiring.

Reprogram is for anyone who has ever felt stuck without knowing why.
For those who sense they were built for more, but keep circling the same emotional patterns.
For the quiet ones who know their pain is real, even if no one else sees it.

This is not a promise of instant change.
But it is a promise of honest insight.
And if you stay with it, a slow but lasting transformation.

Thank you for being here.

I wrote these pages not as an expert looking down, but as someone who has walked through confusion, and found tools worth passing on.

Let's begin, not with pressure—but with permission.
To unlearn. To relearn. To return.

**"Your wound is not your weakness.
It is your opening to everything real."**
— Dr. Saif Qazi

TABLE OF CONTENTS

DEDICATION ii
Preface iii
Before You Begin… 1
Chapter 1: The Lie You Learned To Live 8
Chapter 2: Emotional Inheritance 13
Chapter 3: The Belief Architecture 17
Chapter 4: The Mirror Effect 22
Chapter 5: Energy Is Identity 26
Chapter 6: The Disowned Self 30
Chapter 7: Identity Reclamation 35
Chapter 8: Embodied Identity – Living Like The Self You Just Named 39
Chapter 9: When the World Misses the Old You – Holding Ground as You Evolve 43
Chapter 10: Building Inner Safety – Coming Home To Yourself In A World That Shakes 47
Chapter 11: Triggers – Turning Emotional Pain Into Portals 52
Chapter 12: Identity Scripts – Whose Voice Is This? 57
Chapter 13: Nervous System Kindness – Redefining Discipline 61
Chapter 14: The Future Isn't a Goal – It's a Frequency 65
Chapter 15: Integration – Practicing Your New Normal ... 69

Chapter 16: Aliveness Is The New Success 73

Chapter 17: Creative Power – When Your Truth Starts To Build Things 78

Chapter 18: Fluency – When Healing Becomes Who You Are 82

Chapter 19: Surrender – Letting The New You Lead 86

Chapter 20: Evolution – When Others Don't Know Who You Are Anymore 90

Chapter 21: When Your Life Starts Speaking Back To You 94

Chapter 22: Leading From Presence – Becoming The Ground Others Stand On 98

Chapter 23: Identity Beyond The Wound – Who Are You Without The Pain? 102

Chapter 24: Inner Authority – Trusting The Voice That Doesn't Shout 106

Chapter 25: Reclaiming Availability – Letting Life Reach You Again 110

Chapter 26: You Are No Longer The Emergency 114

Chapter 27: When Stillness Feels Like Progress 118

Chapter 28: Let It Be Easy Now 121

Chapter 29: Returning To The Ordinary – Where The Miracles Actually Are 125

Chapter 30: You Were Always The Home 128

Epilogue: Walk Yourself Home 132

Final Blessing 135

About The Author 137

How This Book Was Born 138

A Note from the Author 140

Before You Begin...

You don't need to be ready.
You only need to be honest.

This book won't ask you to try harder.
It will ask you to try softer.

It won't demand discipline.
It will invite devotion—
to your breath,
to your becoming,
to the part of you that's always known:

There must be another way.

A way that doesn't cost your softness.
A way that doesn't script your worth.
A way your nervous system can finally trust.

If your life has felt like a loop,
this is the interruption.

If your identity has felt like a costume,
this is the undressing.

If your growth has started to feel like strain,
this is the return.

Go slowly.
Breathe often.
And whatever rises as you read

Know this:
It's not a setback.
It's your soul
recognizing itself
in ink.

Now
begin.

Introduction: This Is Not a Self-Help Book

"You're not broken.
You're encoded.
This book doesn't fix you—
it helps you finally hear yourself again."

You didn't find this book.
It found you.
At the perfect moment in your becoming.

Not to make you better.
But to bring you back.

Back to the version of you
that was never missing—
only muted.

You've tried the checklists.
You've swallowed the affirmations.
You've sprinted through self-help
like it was a race to worthiness.

But the ache never left.

Because what you've been searching for
was never a new version of you.
It was a way to *come home*—
to the one you buried beneath
survival, success, and self-editing.

This Isn't a Book. It's a Rewiring.

Reprogram doesn't offer steps.
It offers **safety**.
It won't hand you another strategy to perform.
It will hold up a *mirror*—so precise, so honest—
you won't be able to lie to yourself anymore.
This is where borrowed beliefs unravel.
Where emotional armor softens.
Where the nervous system exhales—
not from instruction,
but from *recognition*.
You won't find slogans here.
You'll find **sacred interruptions**.
Words that don't just *inform*—
they **rewire**.

The MirrorVerse™ You're About to Enter

This book is written in a style I call **MirrorVerse™**—
not a format,
but a *frequency*.

Every sentence is a reflection.
Every pause is *intentional*.
Every question is *coded*
to help you remember
something you didn't know you forgot.

You won't just read this book.
You'll *feel* it.
Like *déjà vu with a heartbeat*.

MirrorVerse™ doesn't offer answers.
It hands you back to yourself.

The truth was always in you—
this book just speaks its native language.

How to Move Through This Book

Don't rush.
Don't try to finish it.
Let this be the first thing in your life
you don't try to **conquer**.

Let it work on you —
breath by breath, line by line.

- Pause when a line stings.
- Revisit the chapters that confuse you—
  they're brushing up against the version of you
  you're about to outgrow.
- Don't just underline what resonates.
  Ask why.

Some lines will feel like memory.
Others, like medicine.

Both are yours.

What You'll Reprogram Here

Not your *habits*.
Not your *to-do list*.

But your **identity loops**.

The emotional blueprints you inherited, not chose.
The "enoughness" conditions passed down like family recipes.
The trauma-informed reflexes your body called survival.

This isn't information.
It's **liberation**.

If you've ever felt:
- *One pause away from peace*
- *One choice away from your truth*
- *One question away from remembering who you were before the world rewrote you—*

This is that *pause*.
That *choice*.
That *question*.

This isn't self-help.
It's **self-return**.
And you're exactly on time.
Welcome to Reprogram.
Not where your life changes—2
but where your life begins to sound like *you* again.

Chapter 1: The Lie You Learned To Live

"The strongest chains are the ones you cannot see—but deeply feel."

You've felt this.

A life that looks full on paper—
yet aches quietly between breaths.

You wake up.

And for a split second, before the to-do list floods in, there's silence.

Not peace—
absence.

A hollow pause that whispers:
Is this really all there is?

It's not despair.
It's not even sadness.
It's something harder to name—
a quiet resignation.

Coffee, reheated.
Smiles, practiced.
Dreams, archived under "realistic."

Comfortable? Yes.
Alive? *Barely.*

You weren't born for maintenance mode.
You were born to **burn.**

To *feel* deeply.
To *author* your life—
not perform someone else's script.

How the Lie Creeps In

Somewhere along the way…
something shifted.

You were handed timelines and templates.
A name.
A role.
A checklist.

You learned how to fold your fire
into **acceptable shapes**.

"Be responsible."
"Be practical."
"Don't want too much."
"Make everyone comfortable."

Maybe it was the ninth time you stayed silent in a meeting.
Or the day you packed away your paints
because spreadsheets paid better.

Maybe it was when you swallowed your truth
just to keep peace at dinner.

These weren't grand betrayals.
They were **micro-abandonments**—
small silences,
self-shrinkings,
subtle rewrites of identity.

Not lies told to others—
but ones whispered to *yourself*.

And in that quiet…
a ghost began to take shape.

The Ghost of Your True Self

You didn't lose yourself all at once.
You *misplaced* yourself—
compromise by compromise,
mask by mask.

Now, a stranger stares back at you in the mirror.
Polished.
Reliable.
Tired.

But the real you never disappeared.

She became a presence.
He became a pulse beneath the noise.

That *you* became a ghost—
haunting your routines with quiet reverence,
waiting in the margins of your life,
whispering from the **MirrorVerse™**:

   "What took you so long?"

What Is the MirrorVerse™?

The **MirrorVerse™** is not fantasy.
It's **memory**.

It's the inner space
where the unchosen version of you still lives—

The one who never edited their joy.
Never apologized for their voice.
Never mistook approval for belonging.

It's the place where your truest self still waits—
untamed,
unfiltered,
vividly alive.

We'll explore it more soon.
But for now, just know:

It's still there.

And it remembers you.

You don't need to become someone new.
You only need to *stop leaving* the one you already are.

The Choice Point

You stand now at the edge of an inherited script.
One foot in fear.
One foot in memory.

And ahead?

A blank canvas—
untouched.
Unclaimed.
Waiting for your truth.

This isn't the moment for grand reinvention.
This is the moment for **return**.

Not to who the world told you to be.
But to who you've always been—
beneath the noise,
beneath the armor,
beneath the habit of disappearing.

Breathe.
Let the fog thin.
And listen.

❂ Sacred Question

If you could live one life—fully, fearlessly, and on your own terms—
what truth would you stop denying?

Chapter 2: Emotional Inheritance

What Wasn't Yours, But Lives in You

> *"Some wounds didn't begin with you.
> But they speak in your voice."*

You've made choices that never felt like yours.
You've said *"I'm fine"* when something inside was screaming.
You've flinched at praise. Apologized for existing too loudly.
You've sabotaged the very thing you wanted—
then felt ashamed for wanting it in the first place.

And somewhere deep down, you've wondered:
Why do I do this?
Where did this begin?
Why does my pain feel older than my memory?

What if the answer is this:
You inherited it.

Not just your eye color or your walk—
but your **emotional settings**.
Your silence. Your fears.
Your inability to rest without guilt.
Your habit of shrinking when seen.

You Didn't Choose the Pattern—You Inherited the Program

You didn't choose:
- The fear of being too much
- The instinct to people-please

- The flinch before joy
- The voice that says, *"You'll be left if you speak too honestly"*

But somewhere back in your lineage...
someone had to survive.

And **survival has a memory.**
That memory lives in your body.
That emotion lives in your nervous system.
You're not broken.
You're encoded.

Emotional DNA

This is **emotional inheritance**:
the unconscious transfer of beliefs, coping mechanisms, fears, and shame—
passed down like family recipes no one meant to hand over.

You may not know your great-grandmother's story.
But maybe you carry her grief in your chest
every time you silence your needs.

You may not recall the rules of your childhood household.
But maybe you still ask for permission to rest.

Not because you're weak—
but because your **blueprint** was shaped
before you could question it.

The Science of What Stays

Neuroscience calls it **generational encoding**:

- Emotional patterns are wired through repetition
- Cortisol sensitivity can be passed epigenetically
- Shame becomes a muscle memory
- Hypervigilance gets mistaken for *"just being careful"*

You think it's just your personality.
But it's your **inheritance**.

Pause: This Is Not About Blame

This isn't about blaming your parents.
They, too, inherited silence.
They, too, were doing their best
with what they were taught to suppress.

**Hurt passes through generations—
until someone is brave enough to feel it on purpose.**
That someone is you.

The Beautiful Disruption

You are the **interruption**.
The **rewirer**.

The one who asks:
"Is this even mine?"
"Do I want to keep carrying this?"

Because while inheritance is unconscious…
healing must be intentional.

You don't owe every pattern your loyalty.
You owe your future your clarity.

What Reprogramming Looks Like

It looks like:
- Saying no with a calm heart
- Resting without guilt
- Receiving love without suspicion
- Not needing to explain why you changed
- Feeling safe in your joy—*without apology*

It's not dramatic.
It's often invisible.
But inside your cells, inside your story—
everything is rearranging.

Final Whisper

Some of what hurts in you
was never yours to hold.

But healing it?
That is yours.

You are not just the echo of your inheritance.
You are the one who gets to choose **what ends here.**

❁ Sacred Question

*What emotions are you carrying that never
belonged to you—
and what would it feel like to finally set it down?*

Chapter 3: The Belief Architecture

Who Built the Walls in Your Mind?
*"You don't live your life.
You live the story you believe about your life."*

You may think you're choosing freely.
But often, you're choosing from a blueprint you didn't design.
You don't act from *possibility*.
You act from *permission*—
subtle, inherited, invisible.

That's what belief is:
a pattern of thoughts repeated so often,
it no longer asks for proof.

Beliefs are the architecture of your reality.
They decide:

- What you think you're allowed to want
- How much love you think you deserve
- Whether success feels expansive or dangerous
- Whether rest feels earned or guilty

You may not even know where your beliefs came from.
But they're running the show.

Your Brain Isn't Broken. It's Loyal.

Your brain's mission isn't *success*.
It's *survival*.

Safe.
Predictable.
Familiar.
That's the language your brain speaks fluently.
Not potential. Not purpose.
You're not wired for failure.
You're wired for familiarity.

The loop may hurt—
but if it's predictable,
your brain trusts it more
than the unknown joy you haven't yet practiced.

Who Built These Walls?

Some of your beliefs were handed to you by:
- Parents doing their best with outdated tools
- Teachers who valued obedience over originality
- Culture that feared too much joy, too much softness, too much *you*

You were never told outright: *"Shrink."*
But you noticed what got praised.
And you adjusted.

Until your personality became a performance.

The Brain Believes What Is Familiar

The subconscious doesn't ask:
"Is this true?"
It asks:
"Have I seen this before?"

Familiar = Safe
Repetition = Truth

That's why we stay in patterns that hurt—
not because they feel good,
but because they feel *known*.

The Loop You Didn't Know You Were In

"I'm not good with money."
"Love always fades."
"I'm too emotional."
"If I slow down, I'll fall behind."

Who told you that?
Whose fear are you still loyal to?

Most of your limiting beliefs
aren't reflections of your truth.
They're echoes of someone else's trauma,
spoken in your voice.

Dismantling, Gently

You don't have to bulldoze your identity.
You only have to start questioning the structure.

Ask:
- Is this belief helping me expand, or keeping me small?
- Where did I first learn it?
- Who benefits when I stay in this loop?

You'll be surprised
how many of your inner walls
are built from someone else's fear.

Reprogramming Begins with Awareness

The moment you see a belief as a *choice*, not a *truth*—
you've already begun to rewire.

This isn't about "positive thinking."
It's about **pattern disruption**.
Not forcing new beliefs.
But creating space for truer ones to emerge.
"Maybe I'm not too much.
Maybe I've been trying to fit into spaces that were too small."
That one reframe
can shift a lifetime.

What a New Belief Feels Like

It feels awkward at first.
Foreign. Almost dishonest.
Like wearing shoes that haven't been broken in.
"I am worthy of ease."
"I am safe being seen."
"I am allowed to rest."
You won't believe it right away.
That's okay.
Belief grows with **repetition**—
and the nervous system learns safety through **experience**.
You're not lying to yourself.
You're introducing a new reality
to the old gatekeepers in your brain.

Final Whisper

You're not wired for failure.
You're wired for what feels *safe*.
But safe is not always **true**.
And familiar is not always **freedom**.

Your thoughts are not your truth.
They're just **tenants** in your mind.
And you—
you are the landlord now.

❋ Sacred Question

> *What familiar loop are you still obeying—*
> *that no longer deserves your loyalty?*

Chapter 4: The Mirror Effect

You Become What You're Exposed To

*"You weren't only taught through words.
You were taught through proximity."*

You are not only a product of what you believe.
You are a product of what you've witnessed repeatedly.
You didn't just inherit stories.
You absorbed **frequencies**.
The fear in your mother's silence.
The shame in your father's tension.
The flinch of being seen too clearly.
The caution in your teacher's eyes when you tried to shine.
Your brain didn't just *learn*.
It **mirrored**.

Mirror Neurons: The Imitation Blueprint

We are born with **mirror neurons**—
neurological pathways that mimic what we see, feel, and hear.

You saw someone suppress their joy?
You learned joy might be dangerous.

You saw someone apologize for resting?
You coded that rest must be earned.

You saw someone flinch when receiving affection?
You began to associate love with exposure.

This is not imagination.
It's **emotional osmosis**.

You don't just become like the people you admire.
You become like the people you *survived*.

The Company of Influence

Your subconscious is a mimic—
hungry, impressionable, always downloading.

It mirrors:

- Tone
- Posture
- Fear
- Language
- Self-image
- Even energy

You didn't just learn behaviors.
You **absorbed identities**.

Not because you lacked one—
but because survival required you to borrow the one that was safest.

The Nervous System Copies Safety

Your nervous system doesn't ask:
"Is this joyful?"
It asks:
"Is this familiar?"

So even if the behavior was limiting—
if it kept you safe, silent, or accepted—
your body downloaded it like gospel.

"Shrink here.
Stay small there.
Don't ask for that."

You weren't weak.
You were adapting.

Who Did You Mirror to Survive?

It might've been:

- A mother who dimmed her voice in front of men
- A father who only expressed affection through sarcasm
- An elder sibling who masked pain with perfection
- A teacher who smiled too tightly for too long

And now...
you mirror them when you least expect it.

In your tone with your partner.
In the way you accept less than you deserve.
In how you flinch at joy because it feels foreign.

Naming the Pattern Is Power

This is not about blame.
It's about **visibility**.

You can't release what you haven't recognized.

This chapter isn't asking you to *rebel*.
It's inviting you to **return**—
to a self that isn't borrowed, edited, or contorted for comfort.

Becoming Intentional With Exposure

You became like those around you—*unconsciously*.
Now, you get to choose it—*consciously*.

Surround yourself with:

- People who rest without guilt
- Friends who celebrate, not compete
- Voices that invite your wholeness, not your performance
- Spaces where truth doesn't feel like a threat

You are still mirroring.

But **now you decide** what and whom.

Final Whisper

You are not just who you are.

You are who you watched.

Who you survived.

Who you mimicked.

But that mirror isn't fixed.

You can turn it toward **joy** now.

Toward **expansion**.

Toward people who remind you of what's *possible*—not just what's *safe*.

❀ Sacred Question

> *Whose reflection have you unconsciously become—and who do you now choose to mirror instead?*

Chapter 5: Energy Is Identity

What You Allow, You Reinforce

*"Your identity isn't just what you believe.
It's what you tolerate."*

There are parts of your life you keep calling *normal* that are quietly draining the very essence of who you are.

The phone call you always answer—
even when your body tightens at the sound of the name.
The apology you keep offering—
even when you did nothing wrong.
The friendship you maintain out of guilt—
not growth.

These aren't small leaks.
They're **energetic votes**
for a version of you that no longer exists.

Where Is Your Energy Leaking?

You don't just lose energy to effort.
You lose it to **misalignment**.

- Saying yes when you mean no
- Keeping peace externally while waging war internally
- Performing politeness while your nervous system screams

Energy is the raw currency of identity.
And every time you abandon yourself,
you cast a vote against who you're becoming.

You're Not Exhausted. You're Leaking.

Your body always keeps score.

That *"harmless" yes?*
A stress signal etched into your cells.

Cortisol rises.
Breath shallows.
Vagal tone tightens.

What you call fatigue…
is just your body whispering:
"We remember what you ignore."

Leaks Become Loops

Most people don't feel tired because they do too much.
They feel tired because they keep betraying their **boundaries**.

It's not the task.
It's the **self-betrayal** embedded inside the task.

The Disguises of Leaks

Some leaks wear the costume of identity roles—
"the helper," "the strong one."

Others whisper as love. Or loyalty.

Because losing them feels like losing yourself.

(We'll dissolve that illusion next.)

They may have been born from love.
But they are fed by **fear**.

Identity Is Reinforced by Boundaries

Want to know who you *believe* you are?
Look at what you allow.

- Do you over explain? → You might not feel believable.
- Do you tolerate micro aggressions? → You might not feel worthy of protection.
- Do you undercharge, overgive, or stay silent? → Your energy may be hijacked by old programming.

You teach your nervous system your identity by what you let **repeat**.

Every "No" Is a Mirror

Every "no" you say is a mirror held up to your past self:
"I don't need to abandon myself to belong anymore."

And every boundary you keep
is a **vote for your new reality**.

This isn't about becoming aggressive.
It's about becoming **congruent**.

Not reactive—but rooted.
Not loud—but clear.

True power isn't in how you speak.
It's in what you **no longer explain**.

Reprogramming the Leaks

Step 1: Locate the loop
What's draining your energy that you still call *"love," "duty,"* or *"routine"*?

Step 2: Tell the truth
How does it *actually* feel—in your chest, your gut, your breath?

Step 3: Interrupt the agreement

A belief only survives when it's practiced.
Stop rehearsing what isn't you.

Step 4: Build micro-boundaries

Not all transformation needs fireworks.

Sometimes, it sounds like:
- "Actually, I won't be able to attend."
- "Let me think about that."
- "I'm no longer available for that version of me."

Identity Is a Feedback Loop

Who you believe you are
gets reinforced by what you **repeat**.

- Repeat burnout → identity: *"I'm just the one who handles it all."*
- Repeat shrinking → identity: *"I shouldn't need too much."*
- Repeat boundaries → identity: *"I am worthy of peace."*

This is how **energy becomes reality**.
This is how **identity becomes embodied**.

Final Whisper

You're not wired for endless giving.
You're wired for **truth**.

Your energy is your truth in motion.
Protect it like it's sacred—
because it is.

✺ Sacred Question

> *What part of your energy is still fueling a version of you that no longer reflects who you truly are?*

Chapter 6: The Disowned Self

Beneath the Roles You Were Praised For
"The masks you wear aren't the lie.
The lie is forgetting you had a face before them."

You became what kept you safe.
The achiever.
The caregiver.
The peacemaker.
The strong one.
The funny one.
The one who never needs.

You weren't faking.
You were adapting.

These roles weren't chosen.
They were handed to you like costumes.
And over time… they stuck.

Identity or Armor?

There's a difference between who you are
and who you had to be to survive your environment.

When love felt conditional,
when safety was scarce,

when attention came only after achievement—
you learned to **earn your place**.

You didn't say: *"This isn't me."*
You said: *"This is what works."*

So you smiled when you wanted to cry.
You served when you were starving.
You excelled while you were unraveling.

And soon, the performance became the personality.

Who Did You Become to Be Loved?

Pause here:
- Were you the golden child?
- The fixer?
- The one who held everything together?
- The invisible one who never asked for anything?

At some point, you told yourself:
"This is the version of me they can love."

But here's the truth:
You are not the version that made others comfortable.
You are the version that's been **quietly waiting**
for your own permission to be.

Where Does Your Body Rebel?

Your mind might say, *"This is just who I am."*
But your **body knows better**.
- A clenched jaw before every "yes"
- A hollow chest in the middle of applause
- A tight throat when no one checks on you—because *"you've got it together"*

Your body is the witness.
It keeps score of every role you outgrew
but still perform.

Role vs. Essence

Roles are what you do.
Essence is how you feel
when there's no one left to perform for.

Roles got you attention.
Essence holds your **truth**.

The roles are tight.
The essence is **spacious**.

The unmasking hurts—
because what's underneath isn't small.
It's *vast*.

This Is Not Betrayal. This Is Return.

You are not betraying your family.
You are not disappointing your past.

You're simply remembering who you were
before the applause and the expectation.

The self that doesn't perform worthiness—
but simply IS.

How to Begin the Unmasking

Step 1: Name the role

What identity did you adopt that got rewarded…
but always felt like a stretch?

Step 2: Name the cost
What emotion has this role silenced?
What part of you is tired of holding it all?

Step 3: Welcome the one underneath
The one who doesn't always know.
The one who sometimes needs.
The one who can feel messy, unsure,
and whole—all at once.

Step 4: Let someone see the raw version
Not everyone deserves it.
But someone does.

Letting your truth breathe in the presence of a safe witness is the beginning of embodiment.

Roles Get Rehearsed. Truth Gets Remembered.

You don't have to try to be your true self.
You have to stop **rehearsing what was never you**.

You're not here to play a part.
You're here to **come home**.

Final Whisper

You don't need to burn your past to return to yourself.
You just need to **remove what was never you**.

You were never the mask.
You were the **breath fogging it up**—
asking to be seen.

❂ Sacred Question

What role did you adopt to feel safe—and how does your body respond when you imagine setting it down?

Chapter 7: Identity Reclamation

Naming the Self You Were Meant to Be

> *"At some point, healing shifts from asking 'Who hurt me?'*
> *to asking, 'Who do I now choose to become?'"*

The masks are coming off.

The roles are loosening.

The echoes of survival are growing quiet.

And in that space—
between what you released
and what hasn't fully arrived yet—
you stand face to face with the most powerful question of your life:

> *"If I'm no longer that...*
> *then who am I now?"*

Identity Is Not Discovered. It's Chosen.

Forget the myth of "finding yourself."

You're not a lost object.

You're an **evolving presence**. *(Print this on a damn t-shirt.)*

Identity is not a search.

It's a **decision**.

And the most authentic version of you?
Isn't the one shaped by pain.
It's the one shaped by **clarity**.

You've Been Practicing Your Programming

Before now, most of your identity was inherited:
- "I'm the practical one."
- "I'm not emotional."
- "I'm always there for others."
- "I'm too intense."
- "I'm not good with money."
- "I have to prove my worth."

You didn't choose these lines.
You rehearsed them into belief.

And now, we pause the script.
We hand you the pen.

The Becoming Begins with Naming

Identity is sculpted by language.

- How you speak about yourself
- How you narrate your mornings
- How you set your boundaries
- How you imagine your future

Speak a new name. Watch the body follow.

The body always believes what you repeat.

This is how the subconscious rewires:
Through **repetition soaked in emotion.**

The Nervous System Needs Coherence

This isn't about saying affirmations you don't believe.
It's about choosing truths that feel **possible**.

Test your chosen identity in your cells:

- Does it tighten your chest or soften your breath?
- If it calms you—it's likely true.
- If it shrinks you—it needs more time.

Truth doesn't feel perfect.
It feels quietly inevitable.

And if your old self whispers,
"Who do you think you are?"
Thank it.
It once kept you safe.
Then keep choosing.

Identity Reclamation: A Living Draft

Try this:

- "I am someone who honors what I need, even when no one understands."
- "I am safe being seen."
- "I am no longer performing for acceptance—I am rooted in truth."
- "I create space, not noise."
- "I am the calm I used to chase in others."

These aren't declarations.
They're reminders to your nervous system:

> **"This is who we are now."**

Let This Version Be Unfinished

You are not etching your identity in stone.
You are writing it in **living ink**.
This version of you may evolve.
But it must be **chosen**—not inherited.
Some will celebrate your becoming.
Some will mourn the version of you they could control.
Let them.
You are not responsible for keeping old roles alive
just because others felt comfortable with your silence.

Final Whisper

Your truth isn't hidden.
It's waiting for your courage to name it.

❊ Sacred Question

> *If you could choose your identity—fully, freely, unapologetically—*
> *what would you now call yourself...*
> *and how does your body respond when you speak it aloud?*

———✺———

Chapter 8: Embodied Identity – Living Like The Self You Just Named

"You don't become your highest self by thinking. You become them by acting like they already live in you."

You've named the self you want to become.

Now, your body needs to practice it.

Not perform it.
Not force it.
Just feel it often enough that it becomes your new normal.

"This is just who I am now."
Or better yet: *"This is the frequency I now hold."*

Frequency Means Rhythm

What is "frequency"?
It's not magic. It's not manifestation.

Frequency is the rhythm of small, daily alignments—
a tone of self-trust you carry into your walk, your words, your yes and your no.

Not loud. Not showy.
But real.

Your Brain Believes Repetition

The subconscious doesn't respond to declarations.
It responds to **consistency**—especially when the stakes are emotional.

- You say "no" when it would've been easier to please.
- You pause instead of spiraling.
- You choose rest without apology.
- You ask for help... and don't flinch.

These aren't small wins.
They're **identity installation rituals**.

Identity = Repetition + Emotion

Each time you repeat a behavior
that matches your chosen self,
your body whispers:
"This is my new normal."

And these repetitions work best
when they're subtle, not strenuous.

The old loop? It fades.
Not because it disappears—
but because you stop feeding it.

Embodiment Is Micro, Not Massive

Forget quantum leaps for now.
This is about rhythm.

Try this: • The way you breathe before speaking
- The tone you use when setting a boundary
- The slowness you allow in your mornings
- The language you catch and rewrite mid-sentence

(*"I'm just tired"* → *"I'm restoring. I've been giving too much."*)

Embodiment doesn't need fireworks.
It needs follow-through.

What Would That Version of You Do?

Ask yourself, often: • What would the grounded version of me do?
• How would my healed-self answer this message?
• How does my whole-self walk into this room?

You're not faking it.
You're familiarizing your nervous system.

Let it get used to peace.
Let it feel safe being seen.

When It Feels Uncomfortable…

Of course it does.
The old self had years of practice.
This one? Just days.

But discomfort doesn't mean it's wrong.
Discomfort often means:

You're entering the body of your future. Stretch gently.

When resistance rises, say:
"Even though this feels new… it's mine.
I don't need to earn it.
I only need to embody it."

What You Say Becomes What You Believe

Your nervous system listens to your words.

- *"I always attract chaos"* becomes choreography.
- *"I'm learning to hold peace"* becomes a nervous system blueprint.

Speak like your future self has already moved in. Even if your voice shakes, let your vocabulary align with your vision.

Ritual Over Reinvention

You don't need a new version of yourself every month. You need a rhythm that reminds you:

"I don't need to be fixed.
I just need to be repeated."

Final Whisper

You are not becoming.
You are remembering.

And each time you act in integrity with your truest self—
you are reprogramming your nervous system to say:

"This is allowed.
This is real.
This is me, now."

❋ Sacred Question

> What tiny, repeatable act can I begin today—
> a breath, a phrase, a pause—
> to signal to my body:
> This is who I am now?

Chapter 9: When the World Misses the Old You – Holding Ground as You Evolve

"They're not all reacting to who you are. Some are grieving who you were when you needed them."

You've changed.
Maybe not dramatically.
But undeniably.

You're clearer.
Slower.
Less apologetic.
Less reactive.

You pause instead of pleasing.
You rest without asking permission.
You speak truth… even if your voice still shakes.

And suddenly—
the world around you starts to tremble.

Evolution Is an Emotional Disruption

People don't just miss the "old you."
They miss who **they got to be** when you played that role.

- Your silence made them feel wise.
- Your over giving made them feel worthy.
- Your suppression allowed their comfort.
- Your emptiness made space for their bigness.

Now? You're not over explaining.
You're not absorbing blame.
You're not bending by default.
And that feels like **loss**—to them.

You Are the Mirror Now

When you evolve, you become a living mirror.
Your calm exposes their chaos.
Your clarity confronts their confusion.
Your boundaries reveal their entitlement.
Your softness might awaken their shame.

You're not trying to provoke.
But truth—when embodied—becomes **confrontation by contrast**.

And when they react,
they're often facing the parts of themselves
they've neglected to heal.

How to Stay Rooted

You don't have to defend your growth.
You just have to **stay grounded in it**.

Try this: • Breathe before responding.
Silence doesn't mean weakness—it means self-command.

• Let discomfort pass through.
You're not responsible for regulating their emotions.

• Rehearse safety in solitude.
When others withdraw, fill your own presence. Don't chase.

• Expect pushback.
It means the shift is real.

You've changed the choreography—and they've lost their rhythm.

Don't Shrink to Soothe

It will be tempting to go back.
To soften the boundary.
To people-please your way out of tension.

But remember:
If the cost of connection is your self-abandonment… it's not connection. It's performance.

You weren't reborn just to re-enact the old role in a prettier outfit.

You can grieve with them—
but don't return to perform resurrection.

The Mature Middle Path

You don't have to cut people off…
But you also don't have to bleed yourself dry to keep them warm.

You can still be love—without being leverage.
You can still care—without contorting.

**You can be kind.
And still say no.**

You can be whole—
without being understood by everyone you once lived for.

Final Whisper

Some will grow with you.
Some won't.

Let that be their work—not yours.

Your only task is to keep walking,
unafraid of your own footprints.

❃ Sacred Question

Who in your life is uncomfortable with your evolution—
and what old version of you are they still trying to hold onto?

Chapter 10: Building Inner Safety - Coming Home To Yourself In A World That Shakes

"Your nervous system isn't asking for success. It's asking for safety."

It doesn't matter how much clarity you've earned,
how many roles you've released,
how bold your boundaries have become—

If you don't feel safe inside your own body,
you will always be one trigger away
from shrinking back into your past.

The Misunderstood Foundation

We've been taught to chase outcomes: Purpose.
Healing.
Achievement.
Peace.

But all of these rest on one quiet, often ignored truth: **You can't grow where you don't feel safe.**

Safety is the foundation.
Not luxury.
Not weakness.
Not "self-care."

It's survival re-coded into sanctuary.

What Inner Safety Actually Means

It's not about always feeling calm.
It's about knowing:
"I can breathe through this."
"I can be with this without collapsing."
"I don't need to abandon myself to escape discomfort."
Inner safety means:
**Your body becomes the place you return to—
not the place you're trying to escape.**

How the Body Loses Safety

Let's be honest.
Many of us grew up in homes, schools, or societies where our bodies were wired for:

Bracing.
Pleasing.
Hiding.
Performing.

So now, even when things are objectively safe—
your body may still be expecting the next hit, rejection, silence, or demand.

The trauma wasn't just in what happened.
It's in what your nervous system had to do to survive it.

Rebuilding Safety Is a Cellular Practice

This isn't about mantras or mindset.
It's about **experiential repetition**.

You rebuild safety by showing your body, again and again:

"I won't abandon you during stress."
"I don't need to fix this feeling—just sit with it."
"We've survived this before. And now, we're healing through it."

Every time you choose presence over panic,
you're not just calming a moment—
you're excavating an ancient survival code and rewriting it into love.

Practices That Signal Safety

These are not routines.
They are **rituals of return.**

- A hand on your heart when shame rises
- Slowing your breath before answering a call
- Drinking water as an act of nervous system kindness
- Saying *"I hear you"* to your own anxiety
- Lighting a candle before writing or resting
- Standing barefoot and reminding yourself, *"I'm supported"*

Each act is a whisper to your subconscious:
"We are safe now.
And we don't have to earn it."

You Are Your Own Soothing Presence

The most profound shift?
You stop outsourcing emotional regulation.

You stop needing others to soothe you, save you, see you.

You become your own:
Safe space.
Steady rhythm.
First responder.
Inner parent.

And from this anchored place,
you stop reacting—and start responding.

Inner Safety Is a Precursor to Power

Because when your nervous system knows:
"Even if this crumbles, I will not collapse,"
that's when you begin to live courageously.

- When visibility doesn't feel dangerous
- When intimacy doesn't feel like exposure
- When change doesn't feel like death
- When solitude doesn't feel like punishment

You're not numb.
You're resourced.

When you stop bracing for abandonment (Chapter 9),
you begin building a home that can't be shaken (Chapter 10).

That's where true power lives—
not in armor, but in **rootedness.**

Final Whisper

You've spent years surviving.
Now… turn the key.

The door was yours all along.

You don't have to keep checking the exits.
You are no longer the emergency.

❂ Sacred Question

What would it feel like to treat your nervous system not as something to manage...
but as someone to come home to?

Chapter 11: Triggers - Turning Emotional Pain Into Portals

"Every trigger is a teacher disguised as tension."

You were calm.

Scrolling.

Sipping.

Disconnected but functioning.

Then a name appeared. A phrase. A delay. And your body went somewhere else—
not forward, not outward, but back.

Not in thought — in sensation.

Your chest? Tight.

Your jaw? Locked.

Your breath? Forgotten.

This isn't an overreaction. This is a reminder.

What a Trigger Really Is

A trigger is not weakness. Not drama. Not dysfunction or fragility.

A trigger is your body saying:

"This moment feels like another moment that hurt."

The scene is new.
But the feeling is ancient.

The Loop Beneath the Moment

You weren't just upset when they ignored your message.
You were eight years old again, waiting to be seen.

You weren't just defensive when they disagreed.
You were eleven, shrinking in a classroom, shamed for your curiosity.

You weren't just jealous.
You were twelve, watching your value compete for attention.

This isn't just now.
This is then, trying to finish its sentence.

The Biology of Echo

When you're triggered, your brain doesn't ask: *"Is this safe?"*
It asks: *"Have we seen this before?"*

The amygdala—your alarm bell—rings on resemblance, not reason.

It can't tell the difference between: A real threat.
And a remembered one.

So it floods your system with cortisol,
short-circuits your logic,
and pulls your awareness inward—toward protection.

Your amygdala isn't broken. It's loyal.
It remembers every time you weren't protected.
So now it overprotects.

Thank it—then gently update its software.

You're not overreacting.
You're overflowing.

Triggers Are Invitations

Not to collapse. But to come closer.
Closer to the places that still hurt.
Closer to the memories asking to be rewritten.
Closer to the self that wasn't seen—but never stopped watching.
This isn't pathology.
It's proximity.
To the part of you still waiting to be held.

Working with the Flare

Don't analyze it right away. Don't fix it.
Just pause.
Place a hand on your heart.
Feel your feet.
Let the breath find its rhythm again.
And say: *"This isn't all of me. It's a part of me that once protected me."*
That's how you interrupt the loop—
not with force, but with presence.

Re-parenting the Moment

The words you needed then
are the words you must speak now.

Not to erase the past,
but to finally answer its cry.

Once your body is calmer, whisper what was never said:

"You're safe now."
"You're not alone anymore."
"You weren't too much — you were too unsupported."

This isn't just self-talk.
This is subconscious reprogramming.

Each Trigger Is a Portal

You don't have to avoid being triggered.
You have to stay long enough to rewrite the ending.

- The raised voice becomes an opportunity to stay present.
- The delayed reply becomes a chance to feel secure.
- The inner flood becomes a path to inner anchoring.

Each time you respond instead of react, you tell your nervous system:
"We're safe now. We don't need to run. We can choose."
And that—
is how healing begins to echo louder than trauma ever did.

Final Whisper

Your triggers are not enemies.
They are exiled parts of you, knocking at the door of your nervous system—asking to come home.

You don't need to exile them.
You need to sit beside them.

Because when pain is witnessed, it becomes a portal.
Not a wound. Not a weight. But a **way through**.

Every trigger is a locked door
with your younger self on the other side.

You don't need to break it down—
just turn the knob and say:
"I'm here. We can go through this together now."

❃ Sacred Question

What part of me still believes that pain means danger—
and what might change if I stayed long enough to hear what it's trying to say?

Chapter 12: Identity Scripts - Whose Voice Is This?

"Not every thought you think is yours. Some are echoes. Some are implants. Some are cages that speak in your mother's tone."

You're about to make a decision. It's quiet. Small. Maybe about rest. Or asking for help. Or saying no.
And then it hits you: a tightening in your stomach, a voice that doesn't sound like yours, but lives inside you like it pays rent.
"You shouldn't need that."
"Who do you think you are?"
"Be grateful. Don't complain."
You freeze. You fold.
Not because you're confused — but because you've been conditioned.

Scripts Are Not Truths

Most of what we call *"self-talk"* isn't born from self at all. It's inherited.

Scripts are the internalized voices of authority, repetition, and survival. They start early.
Long before you had language to fight back.
Long before you could name injustice or emotional suffocation.

You didn't evaluate them.
You adapted to them.
Because safety depended on it.

Whose Voice Is It, Really?

That voice telling you not to rest?
It might be your father's work ethic—weaponized.
The shame when you take up space?
Maybe your teacher's sigh when you were *"too expressive."*
The panic when you're seen?
Your mother's rulebook: *"Attention is dangerous. Be small. Be nice."*
These weren't just messages.
They became identity scripts.
You didn't just hear them. You became them.
Until your nervous system confused them for personality.

Scripts Are Neurochemical Habits

The brain loves patterns.
Even painful ones.
Because familiarity feels safe.

Repeated thoughts fire the same neural pathways.
The more you think them, the more automatic they become.

Eventually:
• Shame becomes default.
• Doubt becomes preparation.
• Silence becomes protection.

But none of them are **you**.
They're just programs.
You are the operator.

Start with the Sacred Question

Before you believe the voice, ask:
"Whose voice is this?"

Then pause.
Feel into the answer.

It may not come with a name — but it will come with a feeling:
Tightness in the chest.
Heat behind the eyes.
A shrinking. A bracing. A learned apology.

That's your body remembering the moment the script was installed. You don't need to decode it perfectly.
You just need to question its authority.

Script Disruption in Real Time

Here's how it begins:

Old Script: *"You're selfish for resting."*
New MirrorVerse: *"My rest restores the world I'm here to serve."*

Old Script: *"You're too sensitive."*
New MirrorVerse: *"My sensitivity is sacred. It's how I feel truth."*

Old Script: *"No one will love you if you're like this."*
New MirrorVerse: *"The ones who can hold me are already on their way."*

You're not arguing with the voice.
You're replacing it with something truer.

Not louder. Just realer.

Rewrite Your Inner Narrator

Try this mirror-writing ritual:

1. Write down the most frequent inner criticism you hear.
2. Ask: *Is this even mine?*
3. Write a new sentence that honors truth, not fear.
4. Read it aloud every time the old voice returns.

This is not performance.
This is neurological rebellion.
You are not talking back to the critic.
You are returning your mind to yourself.

This Is How Reprogramming Begins

One thought.
One breath.
One refusal to rehearse what harms.
You don't have to erase every script at once.
Just stop reciting the ones that bury your aliveness.
You're not here to be a loyal narrator of someone else's limitations.
You're here to become the author again.

Final Whisper

Your mind is not a museum for inherited fear.
It's a mirror — meant to reflect **you**.
So when an old script plays… Don't shout.
Don't fight.
Just smile softly, and say:
"That's not my voice. That's an echo.
And I don't rehearse ghosts anymore."

Sacred Question

> *What belief still lives in your body like it belongs there —*
> *but if you traced its origin, you'd realize…*
> *it was never yours to carry?*

Chapter 13: Nervous System Kindness – Redefining Discipline

*"Your nervous system isn't lazy.
It's overworked, under-heard, and still trying to protect the softest part of you."*

You've tried being harder on yourself. You've tried pushing through, "managing your time," shaming your way into action.

But the truth is:

It's not that you lack willpower.

You lack safety.

Your Nervous System Doesn't Speak Goals

It speaks threat. And trust.

So when you say: *"I'll wake up at 5am and crush this routine,"* it doesn't hear motivation. It hears pressure.

And if pressure has ever been paired with punishment... Your body resists.

Not because it's disobedient—

but because it remembers pain dressed as "discipline."

Why You Freeze Instead of Follow Through

You don't procrastinate because you're weak.

You pause because you're protecting.

- If rest was dangerous growing up, your nervous system sees stillness as shutdown.

- If urgency was praised, slowness feels like shame.
- If productivity was your identity, quiet feels like death.

So now, when you try to slow down or start fresh, your body flinches—even if your mind feels ready.

This isn't dysfunction.
This is protective patterning.

Kindness as Recalibration

What if you stopped calling it *discipline* and started calling it *devotion?*

Not effort as punishment.
But practice as remembrance.

Try this:

- Begin the task slowly. With breath.
- Replace the harsh command with a soft cue: *"We can begin gently."*
- Set goals that whisper instead of shout.

Let your nervous system learn:

"This time, we do it differently. This time, we don't abandon ourselves to achieve."

Re-parenting Your Drive

Discipline rooted in shame creates burnout.
Devotion rooted in kindness creates rhythm.

You're not lazy.
You're in recovery.

Recovery from urgency.
Recovery from conditional worth.

And like any recovery—it requires gentleness, not grit.

Try a Nervous System Kindness Ritual

• Before a task:

Place one hand on your chest.

 One on your belly. Breathe.

Whisper:

"We can go slow."

• After a trigger: Shake out your hands. Move your spine. Let the charge leave your body.

• Mid-routine: Ask, *"Am I performing or am I present?"*

These micro-practices aren't self-care.
They're **rewiring rituals.**

Discipline That Doesn't Harm

Let your discipline sound like:

• "I will rest when I need to. Not when I've earned it." • "My pace is not a problem."

• "I can move forward without punishment."

You're not building resilience by ignoring your signals. You're building it by **honoring them.**

Final Whisper

You don't need another strategy. You need safety.

Not to be harder on yourself—
but to finally become a place your body trusts.

Because when your nervous system feels safe…
that's when your soul starts to move.

❂ Sacred Question

What part of your life still runs on pressure—and what would change if you replaced that pressure with presence?

Chapter 14: The Future Isn't a Goal – It's a Frequency

"You don't step into the future.
You tune into it.
And the dial is emotional, not just logical."

We've been told to chase the future.

Visualize it.

Hustle toward it.

Prove yourself worthy of it.

But the future doesn't live out there.
It lives in here.

Not in your five-year plan—
but in the emotional signature you're practicing today.

Because you're not preparing for the future—
you're rehearsing it.

With every choice.

Every breath.

Every frequency you embody now.

The Myth of "Someday"

You say: • "Once I have clarity, I'll act."
• "Once I'm confident, I'll speak."
• "Once I'm successful, I'll rest."

But that version of you—confident, clear, powerful—
can't arrive in a life that doesn't welcome them **now**.

The future you want doesn't respond to strategy.
It responds to **energetic congruence**.

Are you living in the rhythm of the life you say you want—
or just hoping it will land in your lap once you've suffered enough?

You Don't Attract What You Want. You Echo What You Expect.

Wanting something doesn't magnetize it.
Embodiment does.

The subconscious doesn't believe goals—
it believes repetition.

If you want peace, you must **practice peace**—
not chase it after burnout.

If you want respect, you must stop negotiating your boundaries just to avoid discomfort.

If you want abundance, you must stop calling self-neglect a virtue.

Your nervous system doesn't care what your vision board says. It cares what emotional home you keep returning to.

What Frequency Are You Practicing?

• When you say yes while clenching your gut, you're rehearsing self-abandonment.
• When you delay joy until you "deserve it," you're rehearsing unworthiness.
• When you speak softly so others don't flinch, you're rehearsing disappearance.

And the loop continues.

Not because you're broken—
but because you're faithfully rehearsing an identity that no longer fits.

The Future Is Built from Now

Let's rewrite it.
Not by controlling outcomes.
But by curating **internal weather.**

Try this:

- Speak like someone who trusts their voice.
- Walk like someone whose presence is welcome.
- Rest like someone whose worth isn't earned through exhaustion.
- Create like someone who believes their work will ripple.

This is not delusion.
This is **alignment.**

You're not pretending to be your future self.
You're showing your body it's safe to become them.

Identity Is a Broadcast

Every thought, every action, every micro-choice—
sends a frequency.

And your life responds not to what you perform,
but to what you believe beneath the surface.

So if your external world feels off,
don't hustle harder.
Tune.
Don't chase.

Recalibration Practices

Ask yourself each morning:

- What frequency do I want to embody today?
- What would it **feel** like to live from that space?
- What's one choice that aligns with it?

That's how the future finds you.
Not in grand leaps—
but in subtle energetic congruence.

You breathe it.
You speak it.
You become impossible to ignore.

Final Whisper

You're not waiting for your life to begin.
It's already humming beneath your habits.

The life you want isn't later.
It's a frequency, gently asking:

"Are you willing to become the version of you who can receive me?"

● Sacred Question

> *If your nervous system became your compass,
> what version of the future would it lead you toward—
> and what part of your present would it ask you to release?*

Chapter 15: Integration – Practicing Your New Normal

*"You don't become new by knowing more.
You become new by practicing what you already know — until it no longer feels new."*

There comes a moment in every healing journey that feels… anticlimactic.

The big breakthroughs quiet down.
The deep wounds feel less raw.
You're not spiraling. You're breathing.

And yet, a whisper rises: *"Shouldn't I be doing more?"*

That's the old self —
mistaking chaos for transformation.

But integration isn't loud.
It's holy repetition.

The Myth of Constant Breakthrough

You've been taught that change is dramatic.
Flashy.
Cathartic.
Grand.
But real reprogramming?
It's mundane.
 Rhythmic.
Subtle.

- Drinking water before you're parched.
- Pausing before you people-please.
- Naming a boundary before it calcifies into resentment.
- Letting joy stay longer than you're used to.

These aren't just habits.

They're **micro-agreements** with your new identity.

And they count.

Why Integration Feels "Boring"

Your nervous system was wired for intensity.

For decades, **activation** meant importance.

Now, when things are steady…

your mind calls it laziness. Your body wonders, *"Where's the adrenaline?"*

But this isn't regression.

This is **regulation.**

You're not flat lining.

You're stabilizing.

From Knowing to Living

You know how to:

- Breathe before reacting.
- Question the script.
- Re-parent the ache.
- Tune to your future self.

Now the work is not to **add more.**

It's to **remember faster.**

Integration is not intellectual.

It's cellular.

It's how quickly you return to truth —
not how often you forget it.

Cellular Practice

Want to deepen your integration? Don't seek **new** insight.
Revisit what already shifted you.

- Reread your favorite chapter.
- Speak your mirror mantras aloud.
- Walk like your healed self would walk.
- Put your hand on your heart and say:

*"We don't abandon ourselves anymore.
This is our new normal now."*

Every time you choose presence over panic,
you're not just calming a moment —
you're excavating an ancient survival code and rewriting it into love.

Integration ≠ Perfection

You will still forget.
You will still falter.
You will still flinch when old wounds echo.

That doesn't mean you're back at zero.
It means you're walking with awareness.

The difference now? You catch the spiral sooner.
You breathe into the pause.
You come back — **without shame.**

That's growth.
That's grace.
That's proof.

The Nervous System's Quiet Revolution

Your old self was loud.
Reactive.
Proving.
Performing.
Your new self?
Still.
Rooted.
Discerning.
Integration is not just what you do.
It's what you no longer need to do to feel whole.

Final Whisper

You've spent enough time breaking the cycle.
Now — build the rhythm.
Let your days echo your healing.
Let your slowness be sacred.
Let your rituals be revolutionary.
You are no longer becoming.
You are remembering — on repeat.

❂ Sacred Question

> *If healing no longer required proving anything... what rhythms would you finally allow to become your way of being?*

Chapter 16: Aliveness Is The New Success

*"You weren't born to manage life.
You were born to feel it."*

There's a kind of healing that isn't just about fixing pain.
It's about **reclaiming joy.**

Laughter.

Creativity.

Movement.

Moments that make you forget time.

Not because you're avoiding your wounds,
but because you've finally made space for **life beyond them.**

This is that chapter.

The False Finish Line

Most people heal just enough to become functional again.

They stop the bleeding.

They manage the triggers.

They organize their schedule.

They breathe a little easier.

But something still feels flat.

The colors don't pop.

The music doesn't move you.

The joy doesn't stick.

That's because you're not here to feel *"fine."*
You're here to feel **fully.**
And that requires a new definition of success.

Redefining What It Means to "Make It"

For most of your life, success meant:
- Achievement.
- Approval.
- Control.
- Survival with style.

But what if real success sounds like: • *"I laughed today."*
- *"I felt proud and didn't shrink it."*
- *"I said 'I love you' first."*
- *"I danced even though no one else joined in."*
- *"I made a mistake and still felt worthy."*

These aren't side effects of healing.
They're the **evidence** of it.

The Biology of Aliveness

Your nervous system isn't just built for danger detection.
It's built for **pleasure, awe, wonder, and presence.**

When you're in survival mode:
- Your senses dull.
- Your muscles brace.
- Your creativity shuts down.

But when you're safe?
- The prefrontal cortex lights up.
- Oxytocin and serotonin return.
- Imagination reawakens.

Life **opens.**

You feel the wind again.
The music lands differently.
The food tastes like gratitude.

This is not romanticism.
It's **re-regulation**.

What Aliveness Feels Like

- That moment when your shoulders drop… and you didn't even notice they were tense.
- That laugh that escapes before your mind can filter it.
- That bold text you send because your truth matters more than the outcome.
- That walk where the world feels new — not because it changed, but because you did.

Aliveness isn't loud.
It's **available**.

You don't chase it.
You **tune** to it.

How to Practice Aliveness

Not perform it. **Practice** it.

- Start by inviting joy — not scheduling it.
- Ask: *"What would feel a little more real right now?"*
- Wear something that makes your inner child grin.
- Play the song your serious self-judges.
- Eat with your hands once a week.
- Let someone love you — without auditioning.

These aren't distractions from the healing path.
They **are** the path.

Because the ultimate nervous system upgrade isn't just peace…
it's pleasure without permission.

Aliveness Is Your Birth right

You were never meant to live in gray-scale.
To rehearse safety forever.

To be the most emotionally intelligent in the room — but untouched by joy.

You're meant to sing with your choices.
To sweat. To love. To risk softness.

To **taste life** again — not just process it.

You are not here to be impressive.
You are here to feel **alive.**

Final Whisper

You've been healing long enough to survive.
Now heal to **live.**

To dance.
To play.
To open your arms wide enough that the world fits again.

Let aliveness be your next milestone.
Not productivity.
Not perfection.

Just breath that feels real.
Moments that taste like *"mine."*
And a nervous system that says:
"Yes, we're safe enough to be free now."

✿ Sacred Question

If aliveness became your new success metric, what would you allow today that your past self always postponed?

Chapter 17: Creative Power - When Your Truth Starts To Build Things

"You don't manifest your life.
You author it — every time you choose expression over suppression."

There comes a sacred shift in the healing journey.

At first, everything is about recovery:
- Repairing the nervous system
- Reclaiming the self
- Releasing survival scripts

But once safety becomes your soil…
expression becomes your birthright.

This is where your power becomes **creative** —
not just in art or output,
but in the life you sculpt every day with your presence.

From Protection to Participation

Healing used to feel like a bunker. You needed insulation. Boundaries. Space.

Now, something new is emerging:
Desire.
Curiosity.
A quiet urge to **shape the world**, not just survive it.

This is not performance.
This is **participation**.

What Creative Power Actually Means

- It's not about being "talented."
- It's not about monetizing your gifts.
- It's not even about being seen.

Creative power is when your inside world becomes safe enough to meet the outside.

When you stop hiding what you know, feel, dream, or long for. When your voice stops trembling and starts building.

You may write.

You may speak.

You may mother, design, dance, lead.

The medium doesn't matter.

What matters is this:

**Your truth is no longer confined to your body.
It's becoming visible.**

Creation Is Nervous System Literacy

Why do so many brilliant people feel blocked?

Because creativity requires **risk**:

- Risk of judgment
- Risk of rejection
- Risk of visibility

And if your nervous system still equates visibility with danger, you will subconsciously sabotage your own becoming.

So creative power isn't just mindset.

It's **biology**.

A regulated nervous system is a fertile nervous system.

Your Inner Artist Wasn't Lazy. Just Scared.

You weren't procrastinating.

You were protecting.

- Protecting your sacred ideas from criticism
- Protecting your softness from comparison
- Protecting your heart from the echo of old invalidation

But now? Your art deserves to breathe.

Your ideas deserve to take shape.

You deserve to know what your power looks like in motion.

This isn't ego.

This is **emergence**.

Practices of Creative Reclamation

Not to produce.

To reconnect.

- Write without editing
- Speak before you shrink
- Share something without apologizing
- Make something ugly on purpose — and celebrate it
- Let a feeling become a poem
- Let an ache become a question you bring into the world

You don't need a platform.

You need a **moment** where your truth gets to exist **outside of you.**

Creative Power Is Aliveness With Direction

You've already touched **aliveness** (Chapter 16).

Now you're learning to **direct it**.

Not through force.

Through frequency.

Ask:
- What wants to come through me today?
- What am I done hiding?
- What truth, if shared, would make me feel proud to exist?

That's your compass.

That's your power.

Final Whisper

You've already rewritten your nervous system.

Now, let that new signal become **something the world can feel.**

You're not here to impress.

You're here to **imprint** —

On hearts.

On spaces.

On futures.

Your story isn't just medicine.

It's material.

Go build something holy with it.

❁ Sacred Question

> *What part of you is ready to stop healing quietly and start creating loudly in the world?*

Chapter 18: Fluency – When Healing Becomes Who You Are

"At first, you practiced the truth.
Now, you speak it without effort — because it's no longer a concept.
It's your native tongue."

There comes a quiet shift in the reprogramming journey.

You stop checking your notes.

You stop asking, *"What would the healed version of me do?"*

Because the healed version isn't a future self anymore.

It's **you** — now.

Integration has ripened into fluency.

Your nervous system doesn't just know safety — **it speaks it.** Automatically. Gracefully. Without rehearsal.

This is the point where healing ceases to be something you **do**. It becomes something you **are**.

From Effort to Embodiment

You used to need reminders:
- Breathe.
- Pause.
- Don't abandon yourself.
- Remember the script is old.

Now? The breath comes uninvited.
The boundary is clear before you even speak.
The fear arrives — but it doesn't stay long.

You recover faster, love deeper, and waste less time shrinking.

This is not the absence of wounds.
It's the presence of **clarity.**

What Fluency Feels Like

- You don't negotiate your worth — not even internally.
- You don't narrate your pain to gain permission to rest.
- You don't perform wisdom. You simply **choose differently.**
- You feel joy — and let it stay.
- You feel grief — and let it move.
- You trust your signals.
- You slow down without guilt.
- You're visible — and unafraid.

It's not that life got easier.
It's that you got **clearer on who you are —**
and what you're no longer willing to abandon to be loved.

This Is Nervous System Mastery

Fluency doesn't mean perfection.
It means **capacity.**

- To feel and not shut down
- To pause without shame
- To be with what's real without needing to escape it
- To be triggered — and return, gently, without drama

Your body no longer needs a manual.
It moves with memory — but no longer from fear.

It's not trying to survive.
It's learning to sing.

From Healing Practice to Living Art

You are no longer repeating mantras.
You are writing them with your behavior.

You are no longer processing your past every day.
You are **living the proof** that it doesn't control you anymore.

You don't need to journal to validate your boundary.
You **feel it in your spine.**

You don't wait for peace.
You create it — wherever you go.

Healing has moved out of your head.
It lives in your presence now.

The Power of Natural Response

What once took conscious effort…
is now automatic truth.

This is the new reflex:

- You hear criticism and don't collapse.
- You witness someone else's chaos and don't absorb it.
- You sense burnout and **slow down**, not prove more.
- You see your patterns — but **you no longer believe they're you.**

That's fluency.
When truth moves through you as naturally as breath
not because you're trying…
but because you're home.

Final Whisper

There was a time you clung to every insight like a life raft. Now you **float** — not because you're forcing calm...
but because you know:

"I can handle this.
I know who I am.
I trust my truth — even in the storm."

That's not inspiration.

That's **embodiment.**

That's **fluency.**

❁ Sacred Question

> *What truth have you been practicing for so long...*
> *that it no longer feels like a lesson —*
> *but the language of who you've become?*

Chapter 19: Surrender - Letting The New You Lead

*"At some point, healing stops being about effort—
and becomes about allowing.
Allowing what you've become to move through you
without resistance."*

You've done the work.
You've rewritten the scripts.
You've built inner safety.
You've touched your creative fire.

And now...
the invitation is softer than ever before:
Stop holding the reins so tightly.
Let who you've become... lead.

You Can't Plan a Self You've Never Been

You've spent so long building the healed version of you:

- Practicing new beliefs
- Rehearsing new boundaries
- Catching old reflexes mid-flight

And it worked.
You're no longer in survival.

But now, something subtler is required:
Trust.

Not trust in life's outcomes—
but trust in your own becoming.

The truth?
You can't fully control the next version of you.
You can only **cooperate** with it.

When Overthinking Is Just Armor

There's a voice that says:

- "Plan more."
- "Rehearse your reactions."
- "Predict every outcome."
- "Stay ahead of your triggers."

That voice is not wisdom.
It's just anxiety… dressed as responsibility.

Because control was your first safety.
And surrender now feels like a risk.

But here's what's actually happening:
You're not unsafe.
You're unfamiliar with peace.

Surrender Isn't Weakness. It's Integration.

You are not abandoning structure.
You're aligning with what no longer needs force.

You are not "going with the flow" mindlessly.
You are listening for where the current already favors you.

You are not giving up the wheel.
You're giving up white-knuckling it.

True surrender isn't collapse.
It's a **vote of confidence in your own clarity.**

What Surrender Feels Like

- Saying *"I don't know yet"* — and letting that be enough
- Feeling fear rise — and not rushing to fix it
- Trusting your boundaries — without over explaining them
- Following joy — even when it doesn't make sense on paper
- Creating without calculating its worth
- Moving without measuring every step

You stop trying to be impressive.
You start letting your natural rhythm lead.

The Nervous System of a Surrendered Self

This isn't about apathy or spiritual bypassing.
It's about **safety that doesn't require certainty.**
You don't need every outcome mapped.
You just need to know:

> *"Whatever rises... I'll stay.*
> *Whatever shifts... I'll adjust.*
> *Whatever hurts... I won't abandon myself."*

That is real power.
And real peace.

Trusting the Intelligence Within

Surrender is not passive.
It's **participatory.**
It says:

- "I'll speak when I'm moved."

- "I'll act when the impulse feels honest."
- "I'll pause when the moment doesn't require my grip."
- "I'll release the timeline. But never the truth."

You don't become passive.
You become precise.

Final Whisper

You've spent years surviving, then healing, then embodying.
Now… rest in your own architecture.

Let the version of you that no longer braces—lead.
Let life meet you halfway.
Let breath arrive without bracing.
Let wisdom land without rehearsal.

You are not late.
You are not behind.
You are right on time to stop managing yourself…
…and start trusting the masterpiece you've become.

❂ Sacred Question

> *What would it look like to stop orchestrating your transformation—*
> *and simply let your new self move, speak, rest, and choose for you?*

Chapter 20: Evolution – When Others Don't Know Who You Are Anymore

"People don't just miss the 'old you.'
They miss who they got to be when you played that role."

You've changed.
Not in a loud, performative way—
but in the quiet places.
The nervous system. The narrative.
The space between reaction and response.

But not everyone sees that.
Not everyone wants to.

And so now…
you find yourself in a strange ache:
You're becoming someone new—
but they're still talking to the ghost of who you used to be.

When Growth Becomes a Mirror

Your evolution doesn't just affect you.
It reflects others.

When you stop over-giving…
someone else has to sit with their own emptiness.

When you stop apologizing for your joy…
someone else has to confront what they've muted in themselves.

When you stop shrinking…
they may feel exposed in their own smallness.

It's not cruelty.
It's clarity.
And clarity changes the choreography of every emotional dance.

The Grief of Outgrowing Dynamics

You used to make peace at any cost.
You used to play the strong one, the funny one, the invisible one.

And now?
That version of you is gone.

Not rejected.
Released.

But others don't always know how to meet who you are now.
They miss the version of you that didn't ask for much.
The one who absorbed, softened, spun their pain into peace.

They may say you've changed.
They may say you've grown distant.
But what they often mean is:

> *"I don't know how to be with you when you're no longer performing the role that made me feel safe."*

Staying Sovereign Without Becoming Cold

You don't need to over-explain your evolution.
You don't need to apologize for growing.

But you also don't need to become rigid.

The middle path?

- Don't cut off everyone who doesn't "get it."

- But don't contort yourself back into the role they expect, either.

Practice staying rooted in your truth—**without armor.**
Stay soft, but not shape-shifting.
Stay open, but not over-exposed.

This is what mature evolution looks like:
Being true without being triggered.

How to Respond When People Pull You Backward

They may joke about "the old you."
They may test the boundaries you've now built.
They may unconsciously invite your regression.

You don't need to fight it.

You only need to remember:
Your nervous system is no longer wired to perform for connection.

And if you stay rooted long enough,
those who are meant to meet the real you…
will adjust their rhythm.

Final Whisper

You are not obligated to keep playing a role just because others never learned a new script.
Your presence is the update.
Your truth is the rewrite.

If they can't meet you here,
bless the history—
and keep walking.

You are allowed to evolve beyond what they remember.
You are allowed to be new.

✱Sacred Question

> *Where in your life are you still performing a past self*
> *just to preserve someone else's comfort*
> *and what might shift if you let your new self-lead the relationship instead?*

Chapter 21: When Your Life Starts Speaking Back To You

"The goal was never to become someone else. The goal was to finally hear yourself — clearly, unapologetically, fluently."

You've come a long way.
Not just in healing…
But in **hearing**.

- The voice beneath the noise
- The instinct beneath the intellect
- The rhythm beneath the rush

And now, something stunning begins to happen: **Your life… starts to speak back.**
Not in words.
But in reflection.

Life Mirrors You Differently Now

The chaos you used to attract? **Quieter.**
The boundaries you once rehearsed? **Natural.**
The opportunities that used to feel too big? **Now feel like fit.**

You're not manifesting.
You're **matching**.

Not because you changed everything around you…
But because you changed the **frequency** you lead with.

You're no longer reacting to the world.
You're in a **living dialogue** with it.

The Mirror Effect, Evolved

"Do you remember that quiet shift, back when this began?
When you first sensed your life could be more than a reaction —
but a reflection?
That was the MirrorVerse™ whispering.
And now?
You're fluent in it."

You may not have remembered the name.
But you've been living inside it this whole time.

Not a framework.
A frequency.
Not a method.
A mirror.

The End of Performing Self-Awareness

You're not analyzing every wound.
You're not posting every insight.
You're not "doing the work" as a full-time job.

You're **being the work.**

- Your boundaries are cleaner.
- Your joy is deeper.
- Your reactions are slower.
- Your rest no longer needs justification.

You're not speaking truth to prove growth.
You're speaking it because **silence now feels dishonest.**

Integration Looks Like This

- Someone disrespects you, and you say "No" — not later, but now.
- You're tired, and you rest — not guiltily, but instinctively.
- You feel joy, and you let it expand — not shrink.

You're not referencing healing anymore.
You're living its **muscle memory**.
Your soul is no longer screaming.
It's humming — and **life is humming back**.

*"This is the MirrorVerse™ in motion —
where the work you've done (the safety, the boundaries, the unapologetic rest) stops being practice and starts being physics.
Your life isn't just changing.
It's matching."*

You Don't Need to Remember the Term

Because you've already remembered **yourself**.

This was never about a writing style.

It was about creating an environment where your nervous system could finally **exhale**.

A space where: • Truth flows through your breath
• Decisions arise from the body
• Reflection happens in every room — not because you try, but because you **are**

You've become fluent in your own frequency.
And the world is adjusting to meet it.

Final Whisper

There's nothing more to prove.
You've walked through every hallway of your old self.
You've sat with your shadows.
You've sung to your scars.
You've softened into your strength.

Now, let the life you've built reflect the truth you finally trust.

This is no longer self-help.
It's **self-hearing.**

And the echo?

It's everything you once hoped for — **now arriving in your own voice.**

❂ Sacred Question

What has your life been trying to say back to you now that you're finally quiet enough to hear it?

Chapter 22: Leading From Presence – Becoming The Ground Others Stand On

"You don't need a position to lead.
You need presence.
And presence doesn't come from certainty — it comes from clarity anchored in compassion."

You've spent the last 21 chapters remembering who you are.
Not as a concept.
As a frequency.
Not as a performance.
As a quiet, embodied truth.

And now, that truth is asking something deeper of you:

"Will you carry this into the world — not as a message, but as a mirror?"

This is the beginning of leadership.
Not the kind that speaks from stages...
But the kind that people **feel** when they're around you.

You're Already Leading

If your nervous system is calm in a chaotic room...
You're leading.

If your silence is safe, not punishing...
You're leading.

If your boundaries teach others how to be more honest with themselves…
You're leading.
You don't have to call yourself a leader.
But your presence is already making people feel something.
Let's make it intentional.

Leadership Isn't Influence. It's Integrity.

Forget the metrics.

- It's not how many listen.
- It's how deeply you're living what you say.

True leadership isn't about having the best advice.
It's about being the clearest signal.

You don't need to raise your voice.
You need to raise your **frequency**.

Because what people really follow isn't words.
It's **resonance**.

The Biology of Leadership Presence

Here's what science says:

When you're regulated, present, and attuned—
others around you begin to co-regulate with you.

Your calm becomes contagious.
Your groundedness becomes a mirror for what's possible.

You don't just lead with ideas.
You lead with your **nervous system**.

And that is leadership at its most sacred level.

What It Looks Like in Real Life

- Someone panics. You breathe instead of joining their spiral.
- Someone projects. You don't collapse or retaliate.
- A team looks for direction. You pause, and let clarity rise from stillness.
- A moment of conflict arrives. You choose curiosity over defensiveness.

No performance.
No over-explaining.
Just a subtle signal:

> *"You're safe here. Even if we don't agree. Even if it's messy. Even if you're still becoming."*

That's leadership that rewires a room.

MirrorVerse™ Leadership

This entire book has been a mirror.
But now?
You are the mirror.
People don't need your perfection.
They need your permission — to be human, to pause, to feel, to reset.
And your grounded presence gives that... without saying a word.

Leadership Is Never Final. It's a Pulse.

You'll still falter.
You'll still get triggered.
You'll still forget who you are — sometimes.

But the difference now?
- You return faster.
- You apologize cleaner.
- You adjust without self-loathing.
- You let the moment re-teach you what power **actually** looks like.

That's leadership without ego.
That's presence in motion.

Final Whisper

You were never meant to lead with control.
You were meant to lead with **coherence**.

Let your nervous system be your compass.
Let your silence hold space.
Let your decisions come from depth, not performance.

And when someone stands near you and exhales without knowing why—
You'll know:

> *You've become the ground.*
> *You're not managing impressions anymore —*
> *you're offering safety.*

✿ Sacred Question

> *What would shift in your life*
> *if you stopped trying to influence others —*
> *and started leading from the clearest, calmest, most honest part of you?*

Chapter 23: Identity Beyond The Wound – Who Are You Without The Pain?

"Healing is not just about mending what broke. It's about discovering what was never broken to begin with."

You've done the sacred work.
You've felt.
You've grieved.
You've named your patterns.
You've traced your triggers back to their origin.
And somewhere along the way…
you forgot to hurt.
Not because the past disappeared —
But because your present no longer bows to it.
This chapter isn't about the wound.
It's about who you are when the wound no longer runs the show.

The Addiction to Identity Through Pain

There's a strange comfort in brokenness.

For a long time, your pain:

- Gave you meaning
- Drew others closer
- Justified your boundaries
- Explained your exhaustion
- Gave you something to belong to

But now? That version of you is healing.

And you're being asked to answer a question that healing never taught you how to ask: **"Who am I… when I'm no longer surviving?"**

The Brain Likes Familiar Pain

Let's be honest: Even peace can feel threatening —
if chaos is what made you feel real.

That's because your nervous system was wired to feel **alive** only in tension. So when the tension fades, you might feel numb, uncertain, or unanchored.

This is not regression. This is **identity withdrawal.**

You're not going backward.
You're just no longer fueled by what once defined you.

You Are Not the Wound. You Are the Witness.

You are not:
- The abandonment
- The diagnosis
- The failed relationship
- The childhood imprint
- The mislabel you believed for too long

You are what remained. You are what **remembers.** You are the clarity that emerged once the storm stopped shouting.

Letting Go of the Identity You Healed Inside Of

There's a danger in holding onto healing as a performance. It becomes:
- A new personality
- A brand

- A constant narrative of "how far you've come"
- A subtle addiction to being understood through your hurt

But healing is not your final form.

It's your **portal.**

The goal was never to be "the healed one."
It was to be **you** — fully, wildly, presently — without the old ache narrating every move.

Practice: Curiosity Over Continuity

Ask yourself:

- What do I love that my healing never touched?
- What am I drawn to now that pain isn't my compass?
- What kind of joy feels unfamiliar… but honest?

You don't need to rebrand.
You need to **reclaim.**

The you that was always there —
before the pain became your name tag.

Let Your Aliveness Choose Again

This next version of you? It's not found by digging deeper into the wound.

It's found by:

- Trying things without over explaining
- Laughing without shrinking
- Allowing pleasure without guilt
- Building without always needing to "heal first"

This is not bypassing.
This is **becoming.**

Final Whisper

You were not born to keep retelling your pain.
You were born to **embody the life that pain tried to keep you from.**

Let your story be known — but not repeated.
Let your past be honored — but not re-enacted.

And when someone asks who you are now…
Don't say, *"I'm healing."*
Say, *"I'm here."*

● Sacred Question

> *If your wound no longer wrote your name,*
> *what version of you would finally feel safe enough*
> *to show up?*

Chapter 24: Inner Authority – Trusting The Voice That Doesn't Shout

"There's a version of you who doesn't need proof. Just a pause. A pulse. A knowing. That's not ego. That's inner authority."

You've learned how to survive.
You've learned how to heal.
You've even learned how to lead from presence.
But there's one skill that unlocks all the rest:
Self-trust.
Not the loud kind that announces itself.
The quiet kind that **knows.**
This chapter isn't about finding your power.
It's about realizing it was **never outside you.**

What Inner Authority Actually Means

- It's not needing to crowdsource every decision.
- It's not waiting for signs from the universe before moving.
- It's not being 100% certain.

It's something softer, deeper, wiser.
Inner authority is the moment your body relaxes when your choice aligns with your truth.
Not because it's easy.
But because it's **honest.**

The Nervous System and Intuition

We often confuse anxiety with intuition.
Here's the difference:

- Anxiety says: "What if I'm wrong?"
- Intuition says: "This doesn't feel right."
- Anxiety needs certainty before acting.
- Intuition needs presence to be heard.

Your intuition isn't a prediction.
It's a **permission** — to move in the direction of what already feels aligned.

And your nervous system?
It's the instrument that tunes to that truth.

Why Self-Trust Feels Foreign

You weren't raised to trust yourself.
You were raised to:

- Please
- Perform
- Seek permission
- Avoid conflict
- Be "good"

So now, when your body says "NO" or "NOT YET" or "THIS IS MINE" —
you flinch.
Not because you're wrong.
Because self-trust is a second language you're still learning to speak without an accent.

Practicing Inner Authority

You don't build self-trust by waiting for clarity.
You build it by **listening to subtle yeses — and honoring them.**

Try this:

• Say no before justifying.
• Pause before asking others what they think.
• Check if the reason you're hesitating… is because someone else might disapprove.
• Let your body weigh in: Does this choice bring tension or softness?

Authority doesn't need explanation.
It needs embodiment.

Inner Authority ≠ Independence

This is not about isolation.
Sovereignty isn't solitude. It's **choosing your center—even in a crowd.**

You can receive wisdom without outsourcing your will.
You can listen to others — and still choose yourself.

Because authority isn't about being right.
It's about being in **right relationship with your own center.**

The Shift from Seeking to Sourcing

There will come a moment… You'll stop asking:

• "Is this allowed?"
• "Does this make sense?"
• "What will they think?"

And start asking:

- "Does this feel honest?"
- "Can I live with this?"
- "Is this aligned with who I am now — not who I was trained to be?"

That moment?

That's not rebellion.

That's **returning.**

Final Whisper

You've spent years asking for signs.

For confirmation.

For someone to tell you you're allowed to want what you want.

Now?

You don't need permission.

You need presence.

Let your yes be quiet and rooted.

Let your no be sacred and unedited.

Let your body speak — and believe it the first time.

That's not ego.

That's **authority.**

Sacred Question

> *What choice have you always known...*
> *but you've been waiting for someone else to agree with?*
> *And what would happen if you acted on it —*
> *not louder, but softer?*

Chapter 25: Reclaiming Availability - Letting Life Reach You Again

*"There's a version of you that isn't just healing...
It's ready.
Not to fight or fix —
but to finally receive."*

You've spent years protecting yourself.
Rightly so.

- From unsafe people
- From shame-soaked expectations
- From identities that silenced your body's truth
- From systems that gas lit your softness

But healing isn't just about what you no longer allow.
At some point...
it becomes about what you're finally available for.

Healing Isn't a Fortress

There's a danger in mistaking healing for retreat. You set boundaries.
You name your needs.
You find safety in solitude.

But then...
You stop letting life touch you.

Joy feels too risky.
Support feels suspicious.
New dreams feel intrusive.

You're safe.
But you're **closed.** And that's not wholeness.
That's **residue.**

Your Nervous System Was Wired to Anticipate Threat

So of course, openness feels unsafe.
To your body, reception once meant exposure:

- To rejection
- To misunderstanding
- To disappointment
- To over-giving and being emptied

But now that you're resourced…
You can rewire.
You can reopen.

Not recklessly.
But rhythmically.
Wisely.
Softly.

The Shift: From Guarding to Letting In

Availability means:

- Letting love come closer — without waiting for it to leave
- Letting joy last — without rehearsing its ending
- Letting your bigness breathe — without pre-shrinking for comfort
- Letting your voice rise — without apologizing in advance

This isn't regression.
This is **regeneration**.

Are You Available for the Life You Asked For?

You prayed for peace.
Can you rest in it now that it's here?
You wanted deeper love.
Can you stay soft when it arrives?
You envisioned success.
Can you receive it without overworking to deserve it?
Availability is not passivity.
It's **permission — for life to land.**

Practices of Reopening

• Notice when joy arrives… and track how long it takes for doubt to follow.
• Ask: "What do I fear this moment might cost me?"
• Speak a gratitude out loud — without cushioning it in disclaimers.
• Let someone witness you without interruption.

You don't need to open all at once.
Just stop treating openness like it's the enemy of safety.

The New You Is Worth Being Met

You've done the inner work.
You've rewritten the nervous system.
You've reclaimed your center.
Now it's time to let the world meet this version of you.

- Not the guarded one
- Not the apologetic one
- Not the rehearsed one

But the one who knows:
**"I can handle what comes.
And I'm no longer afraid to let good things in."**

Final Whisper

You are no longer the wound.
You are the well.

And the life that's waiting to find you?
It doesn't need your perfection.
It needs your **availability**.

So open — not all at once.
Just enough to say:
**"I'm not just surviving anymore.
I'm here now.
And I'm ready to let life love me back."**

❁ Sacred Question

*What if your next chapter wasn't about proving you've healed —
but allowing the healed you to finally be met?*

Chapter 26: You Are No Longer The Emergency

"You don't have to scan the exits any more. You've become the shelter."

For years, you moved through life like it was a disaster waiting to happen.

- Always preparing
- Always protecting
- Always adjusting for the worst-case outcome

You mastered survival.

But something has shifted.

You no longer look over your shoulder in every room.
You no longer apologize just to feel safe.
You no longer ask for permission just to BE.

You're not the emergency anymore.
You're the **anchor**.

The Nervous System's Old Role

There was a time your nervous system was always on alert:
- Bracing for conflict
- Reading the room before reading yourself
- Monitoring tone, silence, distance

You became hyper-aware.
Not out of choice — but **need**.

Because when your safety depended on others' reactions...
Hypervigilance felt like wisdom.

But now, your nervous system knows something new:
Peace doesn't mean you're not paying attention.
It means you're not panicking.

You can stay.
You can breathe.
You can choose.

From Reactivity to Rhythm

There's a rhythm in you, now that doesn't speed up just because the room does.

You don't absorb everyone's urgency.
You don't match their tone just to keep the peace.
You don't need chaos to feel relevant.

You hold your pace.
Because you're not here to be **understood** at all costs.
You're here to be **intact**.

Who You've Become

- You're someone who pauses (Ch. 11) before spiraling
- Someone who rests without guilt (Ch. 13), not to prove worth, but to protect capacity
- Someone who trusts the voice that doesn't shout (Ch. 24) — even when others question it
- Someone who sets boundaries that don't require a crisis to be valid
- Someone who walks into a room and no longer leaves themselves at the door

This is not control.
This is **coherence**.

You're not performing peace anymore.
You've become its **pulse.**

Daily Reminders from a Regulated Self

- You don't have to keep checking the exits.
- You don't need to earn your softness.
- You don't have to be sharp to be safe.
- You don't have to apologize for your peace.
- You don't need a script. You are the safety now.

And when the world gets loud again?
You don't disappear.
You **deepen.**

What It Means to Not Be the Emergency

You are not:

- The chaos
- The cause
- The clean-up crew
- The crisis manager of everyone else's unmet needs

You are:

- The calm
- The clarity
- The breath between reactions
- The mirror that doesn't distort to make others comfortable

Final Whisper

You've spent years surviving.
Then healing.
Then remembering.
Then leading.

Now?
You arrive.
No rush.
No armor.
No need to prove your capacity by bleeding in public.

You don't have to brace anymore.

You're home now.

And the emergency was never you.

✿ Sacred Question

> *If your nervous system no longer saw you as a threat —*
> *how would you show up differently in the world?*

―――― ✤ ――――

Chapter 27: When Stillness Feels Like Progress

"You're not stuck. You're stabilizing. And there's a sacred difference."

After years of sprinting toward safety, healing, and understanding — you've finally slowed down.

But in the quiet... a whisper rises: "Am I doing enough?" "Is this still healing if I'm not pushing?"

That's the old self talking. The one that equated exhaustion with transformation. This chapter is here to remind you: **Stillness isn't stagnation.**

It's **integration.**

When the Nervous System Confuses Calm with Danger

Let's name it: Calm used to be a trap. Stillness once meant:
- You were invisible
- You were disconnected
- You were unsafe
- Something was about to go wrong

So now, when your body rests, your mind rebels. It searches for urgency — to stay "in motion." But motion isn't always momentum. And presence isn't passivity. You're not regressing. You're **regulating.**

The Loop of Over-efforting

You used to:

- Prove your growth through productivity
- Explain your boundaries just to feel allowed
- Hustle for peace by micromanaging your triggers

Now, you're choosing something radical: **To let stability feel like success.**

That's not laziness. That's **leadership of the self.**

What Progress Looks Like Now

- Feeling emotion without performing it
- Saying "I'm okay" — and meaning it
- Not narrating every shift to feel validated
- Being with yourself in silence — without needing to prove your healing

This is sacred. This is enough. This is new.

Practices for Trusting the Stillness

- Check in gently: "Am I still growing — or just growing differently now?"
- When no insight comes, trust the integration.
- Let the pause be the point. Not the prelude.

This is the space where **wisdom roots.**

A MirrorVerse Shift

In earlier chapters, we unlearned the lie that we had to hustle for healing. Now we unlearn the lie that we must constantly evolve to be worthy. You've arrived at a new octave — where your calm speaks louder than your effort ever did.

Final Whisper

You don't have to move to prove. You don't have to post to process. You don't have to ascend every week. You can simply be here. Breathing. Listening. Letting your groundedness speak for you. You're not unfinished. You're unfolding. And stillness is how your becoming takes root.

❁ Sacred Question

If you stopped mistaking stillness for a setback — what quiet truth might rise and reveal how far you've actually come?

Chapter 28: Let It Be Easy Now

*"Healing doesn't always have to be hard.
What if ease wasn't avoidance... but arrival?"*

You've walked through fire.
You've sat with pain.
You've remembered what you once forgot about yourself.
And now?
It's time to let things get lighter.
Not because the work is over —
But because **you've become the kind of person who doesn't need to suffer to grow.**

This chapter is permission:
To let it be easy now.

The Addiction to Effort

Let's be honest:
Ease can feel unfamiliar.
Even... suspicious.
Because for so long, effort was how you proved:

- You were good enough
- You were committed
- You were growing
- You were doing "the work"

So now, when the storm calms and peace lingers…
You wonder if you've missed something.
You brace for the relapse.

But this isn't regression.
It's **relaxation.**
The kind that's earned, not explained.

You Don't Need to Be in Pain to Be in Process

You're allowed to grow through:
- Joy
- Play
- Stillness
- Humor
- Surrender

In fact, that's often where the deepest reprogramming happens —

when you're not even trying.

When the body isn't defending
When the breath is unburdened
When the heart speaks softly and doesn't need to shout to be heard

What Letting It Be Easy Might Look Like

- Saying no without rehearsing the fallout
- Taking a full day off — without earning it
- Laughing without checking if it's appropriate
- Letting someone support you — all the way
- Not reading another self-help book this week
- Letting your favorite parts speak louder than your fears

This isn't bypassing.
This is balance.

Ease is not a betrayal of your depth.
It's the result of your **integration.**

MirrorVerse in Motion

In the MirrorVerse, we learned how to feel again.
To reflect instead of react.
To choose instead of collapse.

Now?
We learn how to **float.**

To let the healing hold us for once.
To let joy be the teacher.
To let stillness **move us.**

Because: **You don't always need to "do" the next thing.**
Sometimes, the next thing is letting the good thing stay.

Final Whisper

You're not less evolved because you're not in a breakthrough.
You're not falling behind because you're not processing.
You're not avoiding anything just because it finally feels… light.

Let this be your new baseline:

- Effortless boundaries
- Gentle truth
- Deep laughter
- Sustainable softness

This is not the break between healing and becoming.
This IS the becoming.

Let it be easy now.
You've earned your own weightlessness.

Sacred Question

What are you still making harder than it needs to be —
because ease doesn't yet feel safe?
And what might change...
if you trusted ease as much as you once trusted effort?

Chapter 29: Returning To The Ordinary – Where The Miracles Actually Are

"You don't need a mountaintop to prove you've changed. The real transformation is when your inner peace meets your everyday life... and stays."

There's a part of the healing journey that no one talks about. It's not dramatic. It's not emotional. It doesn't trend on Instagram. It's when life feels… normal.

No fireworks.
No breakdown.
Just breath.
Routine.
Chores.
Laughter that doesn't lead to a revelation.
Stillness that doesn't need to be named.

And this — this is where your healing proves itself.
Not in what you perform,
but in how you live when no one is watching.

Why "Normal" Feels Foreign at First

When you've been trained to expect crisis,
peace can feel too quiet.
Your nervous system searches for a trigger.
Your brain whispers:
"This is too good. Brace yourself."

But this isn't danger.
This is undramatic safety — and it's a skill to let it stay.
Not because you've become boring.
But because you've become stable.

Integration Doesn't Happen on Retreats

It happens: • When you wash the dishes while humming
• When you notice the tension, then soften your shoulders mid-meeting
• When you stop analyzing your reflection and just smile back
• When you respond to a trigger… with a breath instead of a battle

This is how you know the work has landed.
You no longer need the breakdown to prove your growth.
You no longer crave the edge to feel real.
Ordinary moments have become sacred again.

Anchoring the Miracles

What if today didn't need to be magical?
What if: • Making tea was a miracle?
• Folding laundry with peace was proof of arrival?
• Loving someone without analyzing it was progress?
• Being unbothered was a revolution?

This isn't a spiritual bypass.
It's a spiritual landing.
You're not high-vibing above your life.
You're living inside it — with presence.

MirrorVerse in Everyday Clothing

The MirrorVerse taught you to reflect before reacting.
To soften before spiraling.
To choose presence over performance.

Now? It lives in your everyday choices.
Not your peaks.
Not your posts.
Not your next big breakthrough.

But in: • How gently you close the door
- How fully you taste your food
- How honestly you say "I'm tired" without guilt

Final Whisper

The mountaintop was never the goal.
The goal was to come back to your life —
and find that you fit inside it differently now.

Not because the world changed…
But because you stopped needing intensity to feel alive.

Let the day be ordinary.
Let the moment be simple.
Let yourself be here — unarmored, unurgent, unedited.

This is where the miracle lives.
Not in the escape…
But in the return.

❁ Sacred Question

> *Where have you been chasing transformation —*
> *that might actually be waiting for you…*
> *inside the ordinary?*

Chapter 30: You Were Always The Home

*"The destination was never a better version of you.
It was the truest one—quiet beneath the noise,
waiting to be remembered."*

You've walked through trauma.
Rebuilt from nervous system wreckage.
Grieved, released, re-parented, reprogrammed.

You've let go.
You've let in.
You've let become.

And now?

You arrive.
Not on a mountaintop.
Not in a blaze of glory.
But here—
in your breath,
your body,
your now.

You realize:
You were never lost.
You were only buried.

The Mirror You Were Searching For

Every tool you grasped.
Every breakthrough you clung to.
Every chapter that felt like salvation

Wasn't leading you forward.
It was leading you back

Not to the version of you that needed fixing.2
But to the one who was never broken.
Just hidden.
Just hushed.
Just waiting for space.

And now—
you *are* the space.

The Final Nervous System Upgrade

Your body no longer braces.
Not because life grew predictable
but because you no longer see yourself as fragile.

Peace isn't a condition now.
It's a code written in your tissues.

- You pause without guilt
- You speak without shrinking
- You love without vanishing
- You rest without apology

And when the world grows loud again?
You don't disappear.
You return—faster.

You Are the Anchor Now

You no longer need:
- Another method
- Another book
- Another guru
- Another version of you to earn your belonging

You are the anchor.
The shelter.
The mirror that doesn't shatter when someone else throws a storm.

This doesn't mean you're always okay.
It means you're always *home*.

The MirrorVerse Was Never Just a Book

It was the language your body always spoke,
even when your mind couldn't translate.
The frequency your soul never stopped humming.
The whisper beneath the wound.

And now
you don't just read it.
You *live* it.

Every breath is a line.
Every choice, a verse.
Every day, a sacred page.
And you—
you are the author now.

Final Whisper

You are no longer becoming.
No longer searching.
No longer waiting to be seen.

Because you've seen yourself.
Not through judgment.
Not through strategy.
But through a thousand soft returns to the truth:

You were always the home.

❂ Sacred Question

If you never again questioned your wholeness
how gently would you live your life?

Epilogue: Walk Yourself Home

*"You've reached the end of a book
but not the end of your becoming.
Now, you walk not toward answers...
but with yourself."*

If you made it here,
you didn't just *read* these pages.
You *felt* them.
You let them brush against your nervous system.
You let them whisper to the parts of you no one sees
not even you, some days.
And now?
You don't need to remember every chapter.
You only need to remember **who you were while reading them**:
The you that softened.
The you that paused.
The you that stayed, when you used to run.
The you that let joy in even for a moment.

You Don't Owe This Book Your Mastery

You don't need to implement every line.
You don't need to highlight it into perfection.
You **lived it**. That's enough.
Because the real work didn't happen in the margins22 it happened in your *mirror*.

Every page was a reflection.
But you were the real text all along.

YOU WERE NEVER LOST

Just layered.
Just looped.
Just waiting for a rhythm that knew how to unlock you.

Now, you have it.
And it's not in this book.
It's in your **body**.
Your **breath**.
Your **pace**.

You didn't just reprogram your thoughts.
You reprogrammed your *relationship to yourself*.

And that?
That can't be undone.

THE ONLY NEXT STEP

You may be wondering: *What now?*
The answer?

Walk like you're no longer at war with yourself.

Love with fewer disclaimers.
Rest *before* you're shattered.
Ask for what you need — without narrating why you deserve it.

Let presence become your posture.
Let peace be your frequency.
Let softness be your new strength.

And when the old stories try to resurface?
Don't panic.

You don't have to start over.
You just have to return
to the version of you this book helped you remember.

Final Blessing

If no one told you lately:
You are not late.
You are not broken.
You are not behind.

You're just remembering how to be with yourself in a way that doesn't require abandonment.

And if that's all this book gave you?
Then it gave you **everything** it was meant to.

You were always the home.
And now—
you finally know how to live inside it.

✿ Last Sacred Question

> *How would you move through your day*
> *if you truly believed you are no longer a project...*
> *but a presence?*
> (Pause here. Breathe. The answer is already within you.)

Acknowledgments

To the silence that stayed with me when no one else could.

To the questions that kept me awake and slowly became these pages.

To the pain that broke me open, and the peace that waited patiently at the edge.

To every version of me that walked this path,
especially the one who kept going when everything whispered, "Give up."

You didn't write this book, but you made it possible.

To my family and friends, thank you for being my quiet strength and loudest encouragement.

To my patients, your stories and resilience reminded me what healing truly means.

To my teachers and mentors, your words lit the lamps I followed in the dark.

And to you, dear reader,
this isn't just a thank you from a writer.
This is remembrance. This is recognition.
You are not alone.
You never were.

About The Author

Some write to teach.
Dr. Saif Qazi writes to reawaken.
Not with instructions but with **invitations**.
Not with strategies 22222but with **mirrors**.

A family physician from India,
Dr. Saif believes healing is not just clinical
it's **cellular**, **emotional**, and **identity-deep**.

As a devoted **Rotarian** and passionate **social reformer**,
he brings the same compassion to his community work
as he does to his writing and medical practice.

He is the creator of **MirrorVerse™**
a groundbreaking narrative style that fuses **poetic rhythm**
with **nervous system science**, **subconscious reprogramming**,
and deep **emotional resonance**.

In *Reprogram*, his debut work,
Dr. Saif channels decades of listening
to his patients, to pain,
and to the quiet truths hidden behind performance.
He writes not to help you become someone else
but to walk you home
to the version of you that was never broken—only buried.

This book isn't just his offering.
It's his frequency.
And the echo, he hopes,
stays with you long after the final line.

How This Book Was Born

This book didn't arrive with a plan.
It arrived like a breath
I'd been holding for years.

I didn't set out to write a book.
I set out to make sense of the ache
the quiet exhaustion beneath success,
the numbness behind performance,
the silent scream of being *"fine"* all the time.

I began writing like I was writing to a friend.
Then a mirror.
Then a memory.

Each chapter wasn't composed
it was *remembered*.

I wrote between clinic hours,
through soul fatigue,
sometimes in the stillness before dawn…
sometimes in the emotional noise
of old loops resurfacing.

But always from the same place:
a quiet, persistent truth whispering:

> *"There is another way to live."*

And now, I offer it to you.
Not as a product.
As a **presence**.

Not to impress you.
To reflect you.

This book didn't come from mastery.
It came from **longing**.

And if even a single page helps you walk yourself home...
then maybe—
it was always meant to.

A Note from the Author

If you've made it this far thank you. Truly.

Writing this book wasn't just about sharing ideas. It was about remembering. Healing. And returning to the self we so often leave behind.

If even one page stirred something within you, I hope you hold on to it gently.

This book is no longer just mine. It's yours now too.

If it meant something to you, I'd be deeply grateful if you could leave a short review on the platform where you found it. Just a few honest words what moved you, what stayed with you can help this book reach someone who needs it next.

Your voice can carry this fire forward.
And for that, I thank you with all my heart.

With warmth and quiet gratitude,
Dr. Saif Qazi

www.ingramcontent.com/pod-product-compliance
Lightning Source LLC
LaVergne TN
LVHW010226070526
838199LV00062B/4741